SCUFFLEHEADS

Published by

Scuffleheads Inc.

Character creation: Gunnar Oddsson

Character design: Gunnar Oddsson & Chris Kuhlmann

Printed in the United States of America

ISBN No 978-0-692-87435-6

www.scuffleheads.corn

SCUFFLEHEADS

Who Are The Scuffleheads?

Scuffleheads are a mysterious group of eleven highly

educated individuals - along with one a little

less educated - whose sole purpose is to inform and

protect the public from Internet intruders.

The group was established in the new millennium, when

the Internet was expanding around the globe at a faster

than anybody had envisioned.

With more and more corporations connecting to the

Internet,

along with us, the regular Joes, Internet invaders - hackers

saw a chance to disrupt and shut down businesses,

and steal our personal information.

World Governments and corporations wanted to protect

the Internet from these hackers, and with

a direct order from world leaders, Scuffleheads was founded.

The Scuffleheads work with local law enforcement to catch

people who use technology to cause us harm and distress.

The Scuffleheads use high tech equipment to find, and dispose of

computer viruses that harm our communication systems. The

Scuffleheads never use lethal weapons. They use ultramodern,

complex weapons to deal with these nasty little bugs.

The Scuffleheads' motto is simple:

WE ARE YOUR FIRST AND LAST LINE OF DEFENSE

Mr. Blue

Mr. Blue, along with Mr. Green, was the first to join the Scuffleheads.

Mr. Blue graduated from a distinguished military school with majors in computer science and electrical engineering.

Mr. Blue served with the armed forces in two wars, and now he leads the Scuffleheads in fighting Internet hackers from all around the world.

Mr. Blue is an excellent martial artist and a weapons specialist, and he speaks four languages.

MR. BLUE

Ms. Orange

Ms. Orange may be petite and innocent looking, but she's a tough cookie and one not to be messed with.

She has a PhD in social psychology and analyzes the behavior of computer hackers.

Ms. Orange speaks three languages and has a black belt in Jiu-Jitsu.

Ms. Orange

Mr. Green

Mr. Green, along with Mr. Blue, was the first to join the Scuffleheads.

Mr. Green graduated with majors in defense and strategic studies.

Mr. Green did three tours of duty and as a high-ranking member of the Scuffleheads, he's an expert on national policy, military strategy and, how to analyze the threat of international computer hacking to national security.

Mr. Green is an excellent martial artist, and weapons specialist, and he speaks three languages.

Mr. Green and Mr. Blue are best friends.

MR. GREEN

Ms. Brown

Ms. Brown is a general in disguise.
She is very disciplined and organized, and along with Ms. White, she makes sure that the Scuffleheads operate as one unit.

Ms. Brown has a Master's degree in science and mechanical engineering, and she is responsible for the designs of the nonlethal weapons used by the Scuffleheads.

Ms. Brown speaks four languages and is a very good boxer.

MS. BROWN

Mr. Slate

Mr. Slate has a master's degree in
computer engineering.

At an early age, Mr. Slate showed
passionate interest in computers. After
his parents bought him his first computer,
he took it apart in two hours and reassembled it in
three hours.

As a member of the Scuffleheads,
Mr. Slate designs and builds advanced computers
and programs not available to the public.

Mr. Slate is a outstanding marksman
who loves archery.

MR. SLATE

Ms. White

Ms. White graduated with a PhD in physics.

With her devoted love for education,
Ms. White spent four years teaching at a prestigious
university, before she was asked to join the
Scuffleheads.

Her interest and studies in advanced fiber optic
technology, earned her the attention of
Scuffleheads, and now she shares her knowledge in
the fight against computer hackers.

Ms. White is an excellent skier, who uses every
opportunity to hit the slopes.

MS. WHITE

Mr. Red

Mr. Red is a business major who signed up with his country's elite special forces and served his country with honor.

Mr. Red was deployed on multiple classified missions to areas that most of us have never heard of, and most likely never will.

Mr. Red is battle tested, and a weapon specialist.

Mr. Red loves soccer and still finds time to kick ball with his friends.

MR. RED

Ms. Black

Ms. Black joined the armed forces after two years of college, and graduated with majors in computer science and network security.

After graduation, Ms. Black completed two tours of duty in extremely hostile areas.

After her deployment, Ms. Black joined Scuffleheads, where her insight in network security is unmatched.

Ms. Black speaks three languages and is a passionate long-distance runner.

MS. BLACK

Mr. Yellow

Mr. Yellow dropped out of college after one year
of studying computer science.

Mr. Yellow was drawn to the endless opportunities
of the Internet and
regrettably became a world-renowned hacker.

After being captured by the Scuffleheads,
Mr. Yellow joined the team, due to his knowledge
of underground activities carried out by hackers
from around the world.

Mr. Yellow is NOT a martial artist, but with
his big hammer hands,
he can deliver a devastating blow.

MR. YELLOW

Ms. Violet

Ms. Violet graduated with a major in communications.

She worked in the Middle East and Africa, designing and building fiber optic networks for global service providers.

Her experience earned the attention of the Scuffleheads, who recruited her once her employment in the Middle East ended.

Ms. Violet is a competitive volleyball player.

MS. VIOLET

Mr. Rose

Mr. Rose has a PhD in
information technology.

After graduation, Mr. Rose worked in
global intelligence for a government agency.

Mr. Rose was recruited by the Scuffleheads, due
to his personal connections within
the international global intelligence community.

Mr. Rose is multilingual and he
loves to swim.

MR. ROSE

Ms. Aqua

Ms. Aqua graduated with a master's in electrical engineering.

After many years working on fiber optic networks for a major service provider, Ms. Aqua was recruited by the Scuffleheads.

Ms. Aqua speaks couple of languages, and competes in several biathlons every year.

MS. AQUA

So here we are, all twelve of us.

Make sure to visit our website for fun facts

and useful information.

We're taking on new adventures and

we want you to come along and enjoy the

world of advanced technology and the

wonderful world of the Internet.

www.scuffleheads.com

Gunnar Oddsson immigrated to the USA 23 years ago and for the last 20 years, has been building and maintaining fiber optic networks for all the major service providers on the East Coast.

Gunnar's passion is to share his knowledge of the industry with his readers in a very simple and entertaining way, along with encouraging the younger generation to get a better understanding of today's technology.

Gunnar was born and raised in Iceland, where books are still a very popular Christmas gift, and where one in every ten people is likely to write and publish a book.

In Iceland we say, "Everybody walks with a book in his/her stomach".

www.ingramcontent.com/pod-product-compliance
Lightning Source LLC
Chambersburg PA
CBHW041221040426

42443CB00002B/38